THE

BLACK DEATH

HOW A PLAGUE TRANSFORMED MEDIEVAL EUROPE AND SHAPED THE MODERN WORLD

MELISSA PAGE

First Edition: 2024

This book is a work of historical nonfiction and is based on research, analysis, and interpretations of historical events. Any errors or omissions are the responsibility of the author.

Table of Contents

FOREWORD

Tracing the Scars of a Pandemic on Medieval Society

In the mid-14th century, a dark and devastating force swept across Europe, leaving behind more than just graves and ruins—it left scars that reshaped the very core of medieval society. The Black Death, as this plague would later be called, reached deep into the heart of communities, challenging the established order, questioning old beliefs, and forever altering the social and economic landscape. The effects of the Black Death went far beyond the immediate loss of life; it transformed medieval society in ways that are still felt today.

The Black Death was not just an event; it was a turning point that shaped the path of European history. Originating in Central Asia, this deadly disease made its way to Europe in 1347, carried along bustling trade routes that connected continents and cultures. What began as localized outbreaks soon turned into a continent-wide catastrophe, wiping out roughly one-third of Europe's population in just a few short years. Entire communities disappeared, cities were depopulated, and farms were left untended. The economic, social, and cultural disruptions caused by this pandemic were staggering, forcing Europe to rebuild and adapt in ways no one could have foreseen.

At the height of the Black Death, panic and despair gripped society. Traditional medical practices failed to stop the disease, and religious institutions struggled to provide solace and answers. As faith wavered and social structures crumbled, people began to reevaluate their beliefs, customs, and ways of life. In the wake of such widespread death and suffering, a new era began to take shape. Surviving peasants and workers gained new leverage as labor shortages drove up wages and shifted power dynamics. The pandemic thus set in motion economic changes that would challenge the stability of the feudal system and create opportunities for social mobility previously unimaginable for the lower classes.

As this book unfolds, we will explore these seismic shifts, examining how the Black Death not only decimated the population but also sparked profound changes in trade, religion, medicine, and social order. By understanding the impact of this medieval pandemic, we gain insight into how societies cope with catastrophic events—and how, even in times of darkness, the seeds of change and renewal can take root. This introduction sets the stage for a deeper exploration of the ways in which the Black Death shaped the trajectory of Europe's history, influencing everything from the rise of cities and the decline of feudalism to the birth of new cultural and intellectual movements.

CHAPTER 1

The Black Death's Journey Across Continents (1346-1353)

The spread of the Black Death across Europe in the 14th century unfolded with terrifying speed and left a trail of unprecedented destruction. Originating in the steppes of Central Asia, the plague found a pathway westward through interconnected trade routes such as the Silk Road. Merchants, caravans, and ships carried more than just exotic goods—they unknowingly transported a deadly bacterium that would ravage continents. By the time the plague reached the bustling ports of the Mediterranean in 1347, it was already a relentless force, spreading rapidly through densely populated towns and villages. The disease moved with chilling efficiency, often killing its victims within days and creating scenes of widespread panic. No village, castle, or city was immune, as the pestilence crossed social, cultural, and geographical boundaries with little resistance.

In response to this sudden and inexplicable horror, European communities reacted with a mixture of fear, confusion, and desperate hope. Many believed the plague was divine punishment for human sins, leading to religious fervor, mass penance, and a rise in fanatic movements like the flagellants. Others sought to blame marginalized groups, resulting in violent scapegoating and massacres, especially against Jewish communities. Amidst the chaos, some cities closed their gates to outsiders, while others tried to enforce quarantines with little understanding of the disease's true nature. Medical practitioners of the era, constrained by limited knowledge, offered desperate measures, from bloodletting to herbal remedies, but these efforts were largely futile. The initial reactions to the plague reveal not only the limits of medieval medicine but also the human need to make sense of and survive unimaginable terror. This chapter examines these responses in depth, revealing how the Black Death's arrival upended daily life and set the stage for profound societal transformations.

Origins in the East: The Beginnings of a World-Altering Plague

The Black Death is believed to have originated in the steppes of Central Asia, in a region spanning what is now part of China, Mongolia, and Russia. Evidence suggests that Yersinia pestis, the bacterium responsible for the plague, may have been carried by fleas living on rodents native to these areas. Over time, the disease would find its way into human populations, likely through interactions between humans and animals as well as through long-established trade routes that connected Asia to Europe.

Historians suggest that outbreaks of bubonic plague were known in China as early as the 1320s and 1330s. These early cases went largely unnoticed outside the region, but conditions in Central Asia were ripe for the disease to spread. The Mongol Empire, which stretched across much of Asia, facilitated massive movements of people, goods, and animals, all of which could potentially carry the disease. The Silk Road, a major trade route linking East Asia with the Middle East and Europe, provided an efficient pathway for Yersinia pestis to travel vast distances.

The disease likely spread slowly at first, moving from one region to the next via merchants, soldiers, and other travelers. Caravanserais—inns along the Silk Road where travelers would rest and exchange goods—acted as hubs for disease transmission. Here, rats infected with plague-carrying fleas could easily come into contact with humans, facilitating the spread of the infection. The Mongol Empire's dense network of trade routes made it almost inevitable that the disease would reach Europe, carried along by the very arteries of commerce that had once enriched the continent.

The precise path of the Black Death's spread from Central Asia remains a subject of debate, but most historians agree that it first reached Europe through the bustling port city of Caffa (now Feodosia, in Crimea), a Genoese trading outpost on the Black Sea. In 1346, Caffa was under siege by the Mongols, who, according to some accounts, catapulted the bodies of plague victims over the city walls, inadvertently introducing the disease to the city's inhabitants. From Caffa, Genoese merchants unwittingly carried the plague back to Europe, setting the stage for a disaster of unprecedented scale.

Routes of Death: Trade, Travel, and the Spread of Disease

The speed and scope of the Black Death's spread across Europe was accelerated by the complex trade and travel networks that connected cities and towns. Once the disease reached Caffa, it spread quickly across the Mediterranean, carried by merchant ships to other port cities. In 1347, the disease landed in Messina, Sicily, when a fleet of Genoese ships, carrying both merchants and plague-infected rats, arrived at the port. Within weeks, people began dying in large numbers, and the disease spread rapidly through the city.

From Sicily, the plague traveled northward to mainland Italy, reaching Genoa and Venice in early 1348. As Italy's major trade hubs were closely linked to other parts of Europe, the disease spread quickly along established routes. Within months, it had reached France, Spain, and other parts of Western Europe. By the summer of 1348, the plague was ravaging the densely populated cities of Paris, Barcelona, and Marseilles.

The rapidity with which the Black Death moved through Europe can be attributed to a combination of factors. Europe's trade routes were highly active in the 14th century, with goods and people constantly moving between cities. Rats, which were common on merchant ships and in urban areas, carried the fleas that spread the plague. The warm, crowded, and unsanitary conditions in Europe's cities made them ideal breeding grounds for the disease.

Traveling both overland and by sea, the plague moved from Italy into the heart of Europe, reaching the British Isles by 1349. By that time, it had also spread into Scandinavia and Eastern Europe. The disease did not discriminate between cities and rural areas; although the death toll was often highest in crowded urban centers, remote villages were not spared. Everywhere it went, the Black Death left a trail of death and misery.

The geographic spread of the Black Death was accompanied by several distinct types of plague: bubonic, pneumonic, and septicemic. Bubonic plague, which caused the iconic swollen lymph nodes (or buboes), was the most common form. It spread primarily through flea bites, and while it was deadly, it was less contagious than the pneumonic form, which could spread from person to person through respiratory droplets. Pneumonic plague was particularly deadly because it bypassed fleas and was highly infectious, leading to outbreaks that were difficult to contain. Septicemic plague, which infected the bloodstream directly, was the most lethal but also the rarest form. This deadly combination of transmission methods made the Black Death almost impossible to control.

Shock and Desperation: Initial Reactions Across Europe

As the Black Death spread, Europe was gripped by a mixture of terror, confusion, and despair. In an age before the germ theory of disease, people had little understanding of how the plague spread or how it could be stopped. Initial responses ranged from attempts at isolation to desperate and often misguided medical interventions.

For many, the plague was seen as divine punishment for sins, a belief that led to widespread religious fervor. Processions, prayers, and penances became common as people sought to appease an angry God. Some even resorted to extreme forms of self-punishment, such as flagellation, believing that acts of self-mortification could ward off the disease. The flagellants, as they were known, traveled from town to town, whipping themselves in public displays of repentance. These gatherings, however, often contributed to the spread of the disease, as large crowds provided an ideal environment for transmission.

In addition to religious responses, various medical theories were proposed to explain the plague. Without knowledge of bacteria, physicians relied on ancient Greek and Roman ideas about imbalances in the body's humors. Many doctors believed that the disease was caused by "miasmas" or "bad air," leading to recommendations that people avoid foul smells. Some attempted to prevent infection by carrying fragrant herbs or flowers, a practice that gave rise to the popular nursery rhyme line, "a pocket full of posies." Others sought to escape the disease by fleeing to the countryside, although this often only spread the plague to new areas.

Cities and towns across Europe took measures to try to contain the disease, although these were generally ineffective. Some cities closed their gates to outsiders, while others imposed quarantines on ships and travelers. In 1348, Venice established one of the first quarantine systems, requiring arriving ships to remain isolated for 40 days. However, these measures had limited success, as the disease had already taken root in local rat populations, and infected fleas continued to spread.

The initial reactions to the Black Death also revealed underlying social tensions. In many areas, rumors spread that minority groups, particularly Jewish communities, were responsible for poisoning wells and causing the plague. This led to violent anti-Semitic attacks, with Jewish communities in cities like Strasbourg, Mainz, and Cologne being targeted in massacres. The persecution of Jews during the Black Death reflects both the intense fear of the pandemic and the deep-seated prejudices of medieval society.

The arrival of the Black Death brought an overwhelming sense of helplessness. As people saw their loved ones die, often within days of showing symptoms, a feeling of doom set in. Priests, doctors, and leaders were often powerless in the face of the disease, and many abandoned their posts, choosing self-preservation over duty. The speed and scale of the Black Death's devastation created a profound crisis of faith and a breakdown in social cohesion. For those who survived, life would never be the same.

CHAPTER 2

A World In Mourning – The Human Cost

The Black Death's impact on medieval Europe was catastrophic, wiping out an estimated one-third of the population within a span of just a few years. This rapid and massive depopulation left entire villages empty, with fields untended and entire regions transformed into eerie, deserted landscapes. The social order was turned on its head as the scale of mortality meant that no one—neither the wealthy nor the poor, clergy nor commoners—was spared. Families were ripped apart, with many children left orphaned and unable to fend for themselves. Neighbors abandoned one another out of fear of contagion, and the sick often died alone, with burial rites cut short due to the sheer number of deaths. Communities, stretched to their breaking point, struggled to perform even the most basic acts of compassion and care for the dead, leaving bodies to pile up in mass graves and causing psychological scars that would persist for generations.

Amidst this widespread devastation, survivors were faced with the monumental task of rebuilding their lives and grappling with the trauma of loss. Some turned to religious devotion in hopes of finding meaning or redemption, while others grew disillusioned, questioning the institutions that had failed to protect them. The disintegration of families and the collapse of traditional social bonds led to new forms of kinship and support networks. Additionally, labor shortages in the wake of the plague's destruction altered the balance of power between landowners and peasants, as workers could demand higher wages and better conditions.

Death Toll and Population Decline: Counting the Losses

The Black Death's toll on Europe was staggering, resulting in the death of approximately one-third of the continent's population within just a few short years. Estimates suggest that between 25 and 50 million people perished across Europe, a figure almost incomprehensible to modern minds. For context, consider that entire towns, once vibrant with life, became ghost towns overnight, and cities that had taken centuries to grow were left hollowed and devastated. The mortality rate varied from region to region but was felt in nearly every corner of Europe.

The death toll not only affected densely populated urban centers but also reached into rural villages, affecting agricultural production and weakening food supply chains. Certain areas in Italy, France, and England were particularly hard-hit, with some towns losing as much as 70% of their populations. In regions where the plague was especially severe, fields went untended, livestock wandered without caretakers, and food supplies dwindled. The loss of so many lives in such a short period created a ripple effect that impacted labor, economy, and social stability for generations to come.

The plague's rapid and indiscriminate nature made it difficult to contain, especially in densely populated areas where sanitation was poor, and families lived in close quarters. In cities, where waste disposal was minimal and streets were crowded with merchants, artisans, and travelers, the disease spread easily. People fell ill quickly, often developing tell-tale signs of the plague such as swollen lymph nodes, fever, and bleeding. For many, death followed within days.

The scope of population decline was unprecedented, affecting not only the number of individuals in a given region but also the structure of families and communities. The magnitude of the loss created immediate labor shortages, which would later contribute to major social and economic changes. The shortage of workers meant that the survivors, particularly in lower social classes, found themselves with more leverage to demand higher wages and better working conditions. In the years that followed, this shift in labor dynamics would challenge the foundations of the feudal system, sparking new tensions between landowners and laborers that would continue for generations.

Society Torn Apart: The Collapse of Families and Communities

The Black Death didn't only rob medieval Europe of its population; it also disrupted the core structures that held society together. Families were torn apart as parents, children, siblings, and neighbors succumbed to the disease, often within days of each other. In many cases, entire households were wiped out, leaving behind empty homes, fields, and possessions. Children were orphaned, spouses were left alone, and communities struggled to survive as they watched their neighbors die.

The plague brought immense psychological strain, as people witnessed the daily loss of life around them. Traditional family roles and duties were upended; in many cases, there were simply not enough people left to carry on everyday tasks. Survivors had to contend with the trauma of losing loved ones, often without the comfort of traditional mourning practices. The sheer scale of death meant that funerals were abandoned, as priests and families could no longer keep up with the constant need for burials. Mass graves became common, with bodies piled together in communal pits to prevent the spread of disease—a somber testament to the inability of communities to grieve in the ways they had once known.

Beyond the loss of family members, communities faced a breakdown in social cohesion. As the disease spread, fear and desperation overtook communities, often leading to isolation and distrust. Some individuals attempted to isolate themselves in hopes of avoiding the disease, abandoning friends, neighbors, and even family members. Social gatherings, festivals, and markets that once brought communities together disappeared as people feared contact with others. The Black Death's impact on social life was profound: the communal bonds that had held society together were frayed, replaced by an atmosphere of suspicion and grief.

Additionally, religious institutions that had provided moral guidance and comfort were overwhelmed. Monasteries and convents, once sanctuaries for the sick and needy, suffered tremendous losses as monks, nuns, and priests contracted the disease while caring for others. The death of so many members of the clergy left communities without spiritual leadership. This vacuum in religious guidance added to the societal strain, leading many to question their faith or turn to alternative forms of spirituality. For some, the failure of the Church to stop the plague was seen as a sign of divine displeasure, while others began to lose faith in traditional religious institutions altogether.

The breakdown of family and community structures led to a sense of disorientation and despair among the survivors. Without the familiar support systems of family, friends, and religious leaders, many people found themselves adrift in a world that no longer made sense. The loss of family members, coupled with the absence of social rituals to cope with death, made grieving even more difficult. In this period of mourning, European society began to change fundamentally as people sought new ways to understand and respond to their trauma.

The Aftermath: Coping with Loss and Transformation

The Black Death forced survivors to confront immense loss, but it also opened the door for transformation. The immediate aftermath of the pandemic saw people grappling with grief and fear, while also beginning to reshape their lives and communities in the wake of such a monumental tragedy. As individuals, families, and societies tried to make sense of their experiences, new social norms and practices began to emerge.

One of the most significant impacts of the Black Death was the revaluation of labor. With such a drastic reduction in the population, the demand for workers soared. Agricultural estates, once worked by peasants who had little bargaining power, now found themselves competing for labor. Surviving laborers, aware of their newfound value, demanded higher wages and better working conditions. In some cases, they moved to other towns or regions in search of better opportunities, leading to increased migration and social mobility. For many, this newfound bargaining power was the first step toward economic and social autonomy, challenging the rigid structures of the feudal system.

This shift in labor dynamics led to tensions between landowners and laborers. In an effort to maintain control over their workforce, some landowners and governments tried to impose wage controls and restrictions on labor movement, leading to uprisings in several regions. The English Peasants' Revolt of 1381, for example, was fueled in part by the economic pressures following the Black Death. This period of unrest marked the beginning of a broader social transformation as the rigid hierarchies of medieval Europe began to loosen, setting the stage for changes that would continue into the Renaissance and beyond.

Religious beliefs and practices were also transformed in the wake of the Black Death. Many people struggled to understand why such a catastrophe had occurred, often attributing it to divine punishment. Some turned to the Church, seeking comfort and forgiveness, while others grew disillusioned with religious institutions that had failed to protect them. In some regions, heretical movements and alternative religious practices gained popularity, as people sought new ways to understand their suffering. This shift in religious attitudes contributed to the growth of secularism and the questioning of traditional authority, paving the way for the cultural and intellectual shifts that would characterize the later Middle Ages.

The Black Death also left a lasting impact on art and literature. The overwhelming presence of death inspired a wave of macabre themes, as artists, writers, and musicians sought to express the trauma of the period. Images of skeletons, decaying bodies, and scenes of the danse macabre—a dance of death in which figures of all social classes are depicted dancing with skeletons— became common motifs. These works served both as reminders of the fragility of life and as reflections on the moral and spiritual lessons of the pandemic. In literature, too, the theme of mortality and the impermanence of life became central. Works like Giovanni Boccaccio's The Decameron, written during the plague years, captured the emotional and psychological turmoil of the era, as well as the resilience of those who survived.

In addition to its social and cultural impacts, the Black Death also had significant psychological effects. The experience of surviving such a catastrophe led many people to reevaluate their priorities and values. For some, the transience of life inspired a new appreciation for earthly pleasures, leading to a greater emphasis on material wealth and personal fulfillment. For others, the trauma of the plague reinforced a focus on spirituality and moral integrity. These shifting values contributed to a broader transformation in European society, influencing everything from family dynamics to political structures.

The period following the Black Death was marked by both grief and resilience. Europe was a society in mourning, struggling to process the unprecedented scale of death and disruption. Yet, even amid the devastation, new opportunities and social changes emerged. Survivors had to rebuild their lives, communities, and institutions in the aftermath of loss, often creating new social norms and practices that would endure for centuries. The Black Death, while profoundly tragic, ultimately catalyzed a period of transformation that reshaped European society in lasting ways.

CHAPTER 3

Economic Upheaval And The Path To Change

The Black Death's destructive sweep across Europe in the 14th century had far-reaching economic consequences that reverberated through every layer of medieval society. With significant portions of the population wiped out, labor shortages became a pressing issue, disrupting agriculture, artisanal production, and commerce. Fields once filled with crops were left fallow, and the scarcity of workers forced landowners to either abandon their estates or adapt by offering better conditions to surviving laborers. This newfound leverage allowed peasants and artisans to demand higher wages and improved working conditions, creating tension with the traditional nobility and challenging established feudal norms. The collapse of the rigid feudal economic system signaled the beginning of a slow transition toward more flexible labor arrangements, contributing to the decline of serfdom and the rise of wage-based economies.

Trade and commerce, too, were thrown into turmoil as established markets contracted or disappeared altogether. The death of merchants, craftsmen, and traders led to the closure of trade routes, scarcity of goods, and fluctuations in supply and demand that sparked inflation or, at times, deflationary spirals. In response to these challenges, innovative economic practices began to take root. Emerging credit and banking systems, new forms of commercial partnerships, and more sophisticated networks of trade contributed to a gradual restructuring of the economy. The destabilization caused by the Black Death was both destructive and transformative, helping to lay the groundwork for the modern capitalist economy and the emergence of a more dynamic and interconnected commercial world.

A Disrupted Economy: The Impact on Trade and Commerce

The economy of medieval Europe was deeply intertwined with agriculture and trade networks stretching from local towns to distant foreign markets. With the sudden and massive decline in population due to the Black Death, these systems faced unprecedented disruption. The loss of labor caused immediate productivity issues, particularly in agriculture, the backbone of the European economy. In many regions, farmers and laborers who would normally tend to fields were either dead or had abandoned their posts, leaving fields untended and crops rotting. Livestock also wandered unchecked, as caretakers were no longer available, which exacerbated food shortages and added to the instability of local economies.

Trade was also severely affected as major trading hubs became epicenters of the disease, leading to drastic reductions in both domestic and international commerce. Key port cities such as Genoa, Venice, and Marseille, which had been thriving before the outbreak, suddenly became hotbeds of infection, prompting merchants and sailors to avoid these routes for fear of contagion. Trade routes that connected Europe with Asia, the Middle East, and North Africa were virtually abandoned, causing a ripple effect across various sectors dependent on imported goods. Commodities like spices, silk, and precious metals became harder to procure, driving up prices and forcing local markets to either adapt or collapse.

The fear of contagion and the resulting isolationism also led to the decline of market gatherings, which were essential to medieval trade. Weekly markets and annual fairs, which were vibrant centers for buying and selling goods, as well as for exchanging information, became ghostly shadows of their former selves. This diminished the flow of goods and services, further impacting economies that relied on these gatherings. Merchants and artisans struggled as demand plummeted, and with fewer customers, many businesses shuttered. This marked a dramatic downturn for the middle class of traders and artisans, who had previously flourished in the bustling market economy.

The disruption of trade did, however, create certain unintended opportunities. Regions that had previously relied heavily on imports were forced to produce locally, spurring a wave of local production. Some areas adapted by creating goods to replace those no longer imported, fostering a spirit of economic self-sufficiency. This shift laid the foundation for economic resilience that would be critical in the centuries to follow. For instance, while some industries like luxury goods and spices saw a decline, others like textiles and basic agricultural products found new pathways for growth.

Currency Crisis: Inflation, Deflation, and Economic Instability

The Black Death's impact on the labor force introduced significant fluctuations in the value of currency and wages, creating a complex economic landscape marked by inflation, deflation, and instability. In the immediate aftermath of the plague, the dramatic reduction in the labor supply led to widespread inflation. With fewer workers available to till the fields, manage the mills, or transport goods, those who survived found their labor in high demand. Wages soared as landowners and employers competed to attract the limited workforce, creating upward pressure on prices as the cost of labor became a major expenditure for landowners and businesses.

This labor shortage also extended to skilled craftsmen and artisans, who could now command higher wages, further driving up the costs of goods and services. In many cases, governments attempted to curb wage inflation by imposing wage controls. England's Ordinance of Labourers (1349) and the subsequent Statute of Labourers (1351) were among the most famous examples of such efforts, attempting to fix wages at pre-plague levels. However, these laws were largely ineffective, as laborers frequently ignored or circumvented them, finding ways to demand better compensation in exchange for their skills and services. This tension between the need for fair wages and the reluctance of authorities to adjust to the new economic reality underscored the increasing divide between the peasantry and the ruling elite.

In the longer term, the Black Death's effect on currency stability became apparent as some regions experienced deflation. With so many goods left unpurchased due to the decline in population, prices for items like grain, livestock, and other essentials eventually began to drop. The abundance of resources compared to the reduced demand led to an oversupply in some markets, pushing prices down and creating economic conditions favorable to buyers but challenging for sellers. This deflationary trend, while beneficial to some, further destabilized an already fragile economy and complicated the recovery process.

Additionally, the traditional systems of coinage and currency exchange were strained by the Black Death's upheaval. The shortage of skilled miners and the decreased demand for luxury goods reduced the flow of precious metals into the market, affecting the availability and value of currency. Some local governments responded by debasing their currency—reducing the metal content of coins to stretch their supply. This, however, only added to the instability and unpredictability of economic transactions, as individuals had to contend with fluctuating coin values.

In response to these challenges, financial innovations began to emerge, as both individuals and institutions sought to navigate this new economic landscape. One such change was the rise of credit systems and banking practices. With resources in flux, people began relying on credit to facilitate trade and to ensure liquidity within the economy. This shift set the groundwork for more sophisticated financial systems that would later characterize the economic landscape of the Renaissance. The rise of these early credit networks and banking systems was a direct response to the currency crisis brought on by the Black Death, reflecting the human drive to adapt to changing circumstances.

A New Order: The Rise of Innovative Economic Models

The economic turmoil brought about by the Black Death did more than disrupt the old order; it catalyzed the rise of new economic models that would set the stage for modernity. The plague highlighted the weaknesses of the feudal system, particularly the dependence on rigid hierarchies and a largely immobile peasantry. As survivors found themselves in greater demand, the concept of a static, serf-based economy became increasingly untenable. With a more mobile and empowered labor force, the traditional roles of lords and peasants began to blur, creating a more dynamic and fluid society.

In this shifting landscape, many peasants and workers sought independence from the oppressive ties of feudal obligations. As landowners grew desperate for labor, they increasingly offered incentives like better pay, reduced rents, or even land leases to attract and retain workers. This shift laid the foundation for a new class of tenant farmers and leaseholders who, while still working the land, had greater autonomy and control over their livelihoods than the traditional serfs. The rise of tenant farming not only granted individuals more economic power but also fostered a shift towards a market-based economy where land and labor could be negotiated more freely.

The Black Death also accelerated the growth of urban centers, as survivors sought opportunities in towns and cities where trade, craft, and commerce offered new possibilities. This urban migration contributed to the rise of the middle class, a group of artisans, merchants, and skilled workers who were instrumental in driving economic recovery. These individuals, who were less bound by feudal obligations than rural laborers, began to assert greater influence within society. Guilds and trade organizations became powerful entities, regulating trade, setting prices, and lobbying for political influence within city governments. This rise of guilds marked a shift from the decentralized, agrarian-based economy of the feudal era toward a more diversified and structured economy that could support urban growth and development.

In addition, the economic changes following the Black Death helped to foster an environment ripe for innovation. With traditional roles and markets disrupted, new ideas in commerce and trade gained traction. Financial practices such as bookkeeping, credit systems, and early forms of banking became more widespread as merchants and artisans sought to stabilize their incomes and secure funding for new ventures. This newfound financial literacy and the growth of merchant networks contributed to the later development of capitalism, as private ownership and investment became more commonplace in the pursuit of profit and enterprise.

The rise of entrepreneurial ventures also laid the groundwork for increased specialization and division of labor. As demand for various products fluctuated, craftspeople and artisans began focusing on specific trades and skills, leading to a diversification of products and services in the marketplace. In towns and cities, distinct neighborhoods often developed based on craft or trade, such as those specializing in textiles, metalwork, or leather goods. This specialization fostered an environment where innovation and craftsmanship could thrive, and where skills were passed down through apprenticeships and guilds, ensuring that knowledge and techniques continued to evolve.

The Black Death, while a period of tremendous loss, thus served as a crucible for transformation. The devastation it wrought on Europe's economy forced societies to rethink their approach to labor, trade, and social organization. The old economic structures, built on the foundations of feudalism, gave way to a more flexible and resilient system that would ultimately support Europe's transition into the Renaissance. The changes brought on by the Black Death underscored the adaptability and resilience of human societies in the face of disaster, illustrating how even the most profound crisis can lead to periods of creativity and growth.

CHAPTER 4

The Great Social Shifts Of A Changed World

The Black Death's deadly grip on medieval Europe did more than decimate the population; it shattered the rigid social hierarchies that had long defined European society. Before the plague, life was shaped by a rigid feudal structure where nobles and landowners held power over a largely subservient peasant class. However, the massive loss of life created unprecedented opportunities for survivors, particularly among the lower classes. With labor shortages crippling estates and trade, surviving peasants and laborers found themselves in a position to demand higher wages, better working conditions, and even the right to own or rent land. This newfound bargaining power led to the gradual erosion of traditional bonds of servitude, as feudal obligations crumbled and a more mobile and empowered workforce emerged. The power dynamics of landownership and labor relations were irrevocably altered, setting the stage for a social order that was more flexible and less bound by birthright.

This profound social change extended beyond economic shifts; it challenged established authorities and norms, sparking waves of unrest and rebellion. As the traditional power structures strained under the weight of crisis, people grew increasingly skeptical of the institutions that had once been pillars of stability. The Church, already under scrutiny for its inability to prevent or explain the plague, faced growing criticism and calls for reform. Local and national leaders, likewise, were forced to contend with heightened demands for representation and justice from a populace no longer willing to endure arbitrary rule. The Black Death not only sowed seeds of discontent but also paved the way for social and political movements that would later define Europe's transformation, from the Peasant's Revolts in England to the gradual decline of unchecked aristocratic privilege. By reshaping power dynamics and enabling new avenues for social mobility and migration, the pandemic played a pivotal role in laying the groundwork for a more modern and fluid society.

Class Revisions: Changes in Social Hierarchies

Medieval society had long been structured by a rigid hierarchy, where class and social status were determined at birth and rarely altered. The Black Death, however, shattered this established order. With nearly one-third to half of Europe's population decimated, society faced a massive shortage of labor, which became one of the most significant catalysts for social change. The sudden scarcity of workers created an environment where laborers—especially those in lower classes—could demand better pay, more rights, and improved working conditions. This empowered peasants, serfs, and other traditionally marginalized groups, beginning a process of social fluidity that would have been unthinkable in earlier times.

One of the most striking shifts was the decline of serfdom in Western Europe. With the loss of such a significant portion of the population, landowners struggled to find people willing to work the land under the previous conditions. Peasants who had been tied to estates through hereditary obligations now found themselves in a position of power. They could negotiate for better terms or, in many cases, abandon their feudal obligations altogether, moving to cities where they could work for wages. This shift from a feudal, land-based economy to a more flexible, labor-driven economy contributed to the gradual erosion of the feudal system, as peasants were no longer willing to accept servitude without compensation or choice.

The changing attitudes toward labor also impacted the nobility and other elite classes. As serfs and laborers gained more autonomy, the power of the nobility—who had long relied on their labor to maintain wealth and status—began to weaken. Many nobles faced financial ruin as they struggled to adapt to the new economy, where labor was scarce and workers demanded payment rather than lifelong servitude. Some landowners were forced to offer long-term leases or even sell parts of their estates to peasants, a practice that was virtually unheard of before the plague. This redistribution of land allowed some peasants to acquire property, elevating them from the lowest social ranks and blurring the distinctions between classes.

Guilds, which were powerful organizations in medieval towns and cities, also evolved during this period. The decline in population meant that guild members could wield more influence, and membership in a guild became increasingly valuable. As a result, artisans and craftsmen gained social status, and guilds began to play a more central role in urban governance. Guild leaders often acted as representatives of the middle class, which was growing in both size and influence. This shift marked the beginnings of a new social order where wealth and skill, rather than birthright, became increasingly important markers of social status.

In sum, the Black Death's impact on social hierarchies brought about a more fluid and dynamic society. The rigid feudal distinctions between nobility, clergy, and peasantry began to break down, allowing for a redefined social order that laid the groundwork for the emergence of the modern middle class and more democratic ideals.

Mobility and Migration: New Opportunities and Freedoms

The massive population loss from the Black Death created a new phenomenon of physical and social mobility, reshaping the very fabric of medieval Europe. Before the plague, most people were tied to their place of birth, with social and economic structures firmly binding individuals to their family estates or guilds. However, as the population dwindled and the demand for labor skyrocketed, mobility became a defining feature of post-plague society.

Many peasants seized the opportunity to leave their villages and move to urban centers, where they could find better wages and improved living conditions. Towns and cities, which were previously controlled by tight-knit guilds and merchant families, suddenly found themselves in need of labor, attracting workers from the countryside. This influx of new residents sparked urban growth, transforming many medieval cities into bustling hubs of trade and industry. The cities that could attract the most labor often prospered, as new businesses and industries flourished in response to the demand for goods and services. This migration was one of the early indicators of the shift toward urbanization that would define Europe's later development.

The newfound freedom of movement also allowed people to pursue opportunities across regional and even national borders. For the first time, many individuals were able to choose where they lived and worked based on economic opportunities rather than the dictates of feudal lords. This mobility also fostered the spread of ideas and cultures, contributing to a greater exchange of knowledge, skills, and practices across Europe. As laborers moved from one region to another, they brought with them not only their skills but also their customs, beliefs, and innovations. This exchange helped break down the parochialism that had previously characterized medieval society, giving rise to a more cosmopolitan worldview.

Migration also had an impact on the church, as clergy were often among the few literate members of society and were essential for recording births, deaths, and property transactions. The death toll among clergy was high, leading to a shortage of trained priests and scholars. This shortage prompted the recruitment of clergy from distant regions, bringing new perspectives and sometimes even new theological ideas to different parts of Europe. The movement of clergy and scholars across regions helped lay the groundwork for a more interconnected intellectual community, which would later flourish during the Renaissance.

In addition, the increased mobility provided individuals with a sense of personal freedom that had previously been unimaginable. With feudal restrictions easing, people could make choices about their own futures, which was especially empowering for younger generations. This sense of agency allowed for a culture of experimentation, as individuals were no longer bound to the customs and expectations of their local communities. The possibility of social advancement through migration and economic participation introduced new opportunities for self-determination, subtly altering the mindset of the population and setting the stage for future social movements.

Questioning Power: Skepticism Towards Authority

The Black Death's devastation led many survivors to question the institutions that had previously held unquestioned authority. The traditional pillars of medieval life—the church, the nobility, and local governments—found their authority increasingly challenged as people sought explanations and reassurances in the face of so much suffering. This skepticism toward established authorities contributed to a new era of critical thought and reform, eventually giving rise to major cultural and religious shifts across Europe.

The church, in particular, found itself under intense scrutiny. As the plague ravaged towns and villages, clergy members were often unable to provide the spiritual and physical aid people desperately sought. Some clergy fled, while others perished in large numbers, leaving many communities without spiritual guidance. This failure to protect the faithful led to disillusionment among the laity, who began to question the power and effectiveness of the church. The inability of church leaders to explain the cause of the plague— some of whom attributed it to divine punishment or supernatural forces—further eroded the church's credibility. In some regions, resentment toward the clergy boiled over, and anti-clericalism grew as people became more critical of church doctrines and practices.

This disillusionment fostered an environment where heretical movements, which had been suppressed for centuries, could gain traction. Groups that had previously questioned church practices found a growing audience among the populace, leading to increased support for ideas that challenged the established religious order. These heretical movements not only weakened the church's grip on the people but also laid the foundation for the religious reformation that would transform Europe in the following centuries.

Nobles and local authorities also faced growing criticism. The nobility's reliance on traditional feudal rights and privileges came under attack, as peasants who had gained new leverage in the labor market were no longer willing to endure oppressive taxes and duties. Peasant revolts became increasingly common, with uprisings like the 1381 English Peasants' Revolt serving as powerful symbols of resistance against the ruling class. These revolts were often brutally suppressed, but they nonetheless signaled a new willingness among the lower classes to confront the nobility and demand change. The nobility's inability to suppress these movements completely indicated a shift in the balance of power and a growing sense of solidarity among the working classes.

The skepticism toward authority extended to the very structure of local governments and their ability to provide effective leadership. As towns and cities grew, the demand for local governance that represented the interests of the middle and lower classes increased. Merchant guilds, trade associations, and other organizations began to wield significant influence in local politics, often challenging the traditional ruling elite. These developments signaled the beginning of a more participatory political culture, one in which power was more widely distributed and subject to scrutiny. This gradual democratization of local governance laid the groundwork for future political developments that would culminate in the rise of more democratic societies.

The critical mindset that developed in response to the Black Death laid the foundation for the intellectual and cultural transformations that would come with the Renaissance and Reformation. The challenge to traditional authorities, the questioning of long-held beliefs, and the desire for reform all contributed to a society more open to new ideas and ways of thinking. In this way, the social skepticism that arose in the aftermath of the Black Death played a crucial role in shaping the intellectual currents of the modern world.

CHAPTER 5

The Birth Of The City-State

The Black Death's legacy extended beyond death and loss; it acted as a catalyst for far-reaching change, accelerating the rise of the city-state across Europe. As populations dwindled and feudal strongholds weakened, urban centers began to emerge as hubs of resilience and renewal. In the wake of the plague, many rural communities saw mass migration toward cities, where survivors sought refuge, work, and new opportunities. These burgeoning urban centers offered a fresh alternative to the rigid structures of feudalism, providing citizens with freedoms and incentives unheard of in the countryside. As new towns sprang up and existing cities expanded, they grew into centers of political, cultural, and economic influence. City-states such as Venice, Florence, and other Italian communes emerged as formidable powers, establishing laws, civic institutions, and governance structures that allowed them to operate with autonomy and influence far beyond their borders. This urbanization reshaped the political map, giving rise to a more diversified distribution of power.

The rise of the city-state was accompanied by a fundamental rethinking of urban life. Planners and leaders took lessons from the plague's devastation, improving sanitation systems, public health measures, and community organization to mitigate future crises. Socially, city life fostered an environment where merit and innovation could flourish, eroding some of the rigid boundaries between classes and creating pathways for social mobility. At the heart of this transformation were the merchants and middle class, who formed the backbone of these new economies. Through trade, commerce, and financial innovation, they amassed wealth and influence, leading to the emergence of a powerful bourgeoisie that shaped economic policies, patronized the arts, and championed the spread of knowledge and culture.

Urbanization Takes Root: New and Growing Cities

Before the Black Death, Europe was largely a rural society, with the majority of the population living in small villages, working the land as peasants under the feudal system. Urbanization was slow, and cities were relatively small, often centered around monasteries, castles, or local trade hubs. However, the profound demographic shifts caused by the Black Death—the loss of up to half of Europe's population—accelerated the process of urbanization. With labor in short supply, the surviving population flocked to urban centers in search of new opportunities, resulting in a surge in the growth and importance of cities.

The post-plague period saw a dramatic shift in the patterns of settlement and land use. Large rural estates, once dominated by the nobility, now faced labor shortages. As peasants left the countryside for cities, the growth of towns and urban centers became inevitable. Over time, the once-small towns began to expand rapidly, transforming into important hubs of commerce, governance, and culture. Cities like Florence, Venice, Milan, and Genoa began to rise in prominence, while old cities, previously overshadowed by feudalism's agrarian-based economy, grew rapidly as new trade routes opened up and the supply of labor moved into the urban environment.

Many of these growing cities were located on the coast or along major trade routes, facilitating their access to international markets. As a result, they became vibrant centers of trade and culture, attracting merchants, artisans, scholars, and a new, more cosmopolitan class of citizens. This urbanization was not just a result of population shifts but also reflected changing economic needs. As people moved into cities, they brought new skills, and as industries diversified, towns became increasingly self-sustaining economic units. Cities such as Venice and Florence, for instance, became international trade centers, contributing to the rise of a new merchant class that would dominate the economic landscape for centuries to come.

This urbanization also marked the emergence of the city-state—a city that not only governed itself but also often ruled over surrounding territories. The city-state model became a defining feature of post-plague Europe, especially in Italy, where it gave rise to powerful political entities such as the Republic of Venice, the Duchy of Milan, and the Papal States. These city-states had their own political systems, currencies, and economies, and while they shared some cultural traits, they also fostered a sense of local autonomy and identity that contrasted with the more centralized authority of medieval kingdoms.

By the end of the 14th century, the explosion of city-states had already begun to change the political landscape of Europe. These cities were often fiercely independent, driven by the desire to maintain control over their own destiny. They established complex systems of governance, ranging from oligarchies dominated by wealthy families to republics with elected leaders. In this environment, competition between city-states was fierce, but it also led to a flourishing of art, science, and political philosophy that would come to define the Renaissance.

Rethinking City Life: Urban Planning and Architecture

The growth of cities and the rise of city-states brought with it new challenges—particularly when it came to urban planning and architecture. Medieval cities had been organic in their development, with narrow, winding streets, buildings crowded together in haphazard ways, and little regard for overall infrastructure. However, the demands of an expanding population and the need for efficient trade and governance forced city planners and leaders to rethink the structure of their urban environments.

With the influx of new people and wealth into cities, there was a pressing need for organized urban planning to ensure that these cities could function efficiently and accommodate growing populations. In many of the new city-states, urban planning became a priority. Streets were widened, new marketplaces and town squares were constructed, and public works like bridges and fortifications were built to improve the functionality and security of the city. The layout of many Italian cities, including Florence and Venice, reflected a concerted effort to create more accessible and organized urban spaces.

The development of town squares, or piazzas, became a hallmark of urban architecture during this period. These open spaces were not only centers for trade but also for public gatherings, political discourse, and religious observance. The centrality of the piazza in Italian cities like Florence and Venice demonstrated the importance of public life in these emerging urban centers. The city square was where citizens could engage with one another, with their leaders, and with their culture. This physical manifestation of civic pride and political engagement would become a cornerstone of Renaissance urban design.

Architecture itself also experienced a revolution during this period. Before the Black Death, architectural styles in Europe were mostly limited to Romanesque and Gothic designs, which were characterized by their heavy, vertical structures. In the wake of the plague, however, there was a renewed interest in the classical styles of ancient Rome and Greece. This shift in architectural tastes would culminate in the Renaissance, but its roots can be traced to the post-plague period when architects and builders began to experiment with more open, balanced designs that incorporated classical ideals.

Buildings began to emphasize symmetry, proportion, and the use of columns and arches—hallmarks of Roman architecture.

The new architectural style was not just a matter of aesthetics. It reflected a broader philosophical shift toward humanism, which sought to revive the intellectual and cultural achievements of the ancient world. Architects like Filippo Brunelleschi, who designed the iconic dome of the Florence Cathedral, and Leon Battista Alberti, who wrote extensively on urban planning, were key figures in this architectural transformation. Their work represented a break from the medieval past and a move toward a more human-centered view of the built environment.

As the city grew in importance, so did the need for new types of buildings. The rise of powerful merchant families and the wealth generated by international trade led to the construction of grand palaces, which reflected the status and influence of their owners. These palaces often featured open courtyards, intricate facades, and decorative elements that emphasized the family's wealth and taste. The Medici family in Florence, for example, commissioned some of the most spectacular buildings of the time, such as the Palazzo Medici, which symbolized the power of banking and commerce in the city.

The transformation of urban space and architecture was also driven by the increasing importance of public institutions. Churches, town halls, and guild halls were built to reflect the growing influence of civic and religious life in the city-state. The churches, in particular, became monumental in scale, such as the Basilica di San Lorenzo in Florence, which became a symbol of both religious devotion and civic pride.

Merchants and the Middle Class: Foundations of a New Economy

The rise of cities and city-states during the post-Black Death era was inextricably linked to the rise of a new economic class: the merchant class. The collapse of the old feudal system and the mobility provided by urbanization allowed merchants to become the driving force behind Europe's new economic order.

Before the plague, much of Europe's economy was based on agriculture, with wealth and power concentrated in the hands of the land-owning nobility. However, as the Black Death decimated the population, the traditional feudal system began to erode. The survivors, particularly in urban areas, found that they had greater negotiating power in the labor market. Wages increased, and more opportunities opened up for skilled workers and tradespeople to earn money and build wealth. This allowed the merchant class to thrive.

Merchants were not merely traders of goods; they were also financiers, investors, and shapers of economic policy. The growth of long-distance trade, both within Europe and with the rest of the world, brought a surge of wealth to cities that could control key trade routes. Venice, with its strategic location in the Mediterranean, became a dominant player in global trade, controlling much of the trade between Europe and the East. The city's merchant families, like the infamous Medici family of Florence, accumulated vast fortunes and used their wealth to influence both politics and culture.

In this new economy, wealth was increasingly tied to commerce and the flow of capital rather than to land ownership. This shift helped establish the foundations of capitalism, where merchants and bankers played crucial roles in the creation of wealth. The banking systems established in cities like Florence provided the necessary capital for enterprises to grow, and these cities began to develop sophisticated financial instruments, such as letters of credit and bills of exchange, to facilitate international trade.

The influence of merchants also played a critical role in the development of early banking systems. Italian city-states like Florence and Venice were home to some of the first banking institutions in Europe. The Medici Bank, founded by Giovanni di Bicci de' Medici in the 14th century, was one of the most successful banking houses of the period, and it would go on to influence the financial systems of Renaissance Europe. The growth of banking in the post-plague period was directly tied to the rise of the merchant class, which, with its increasing wealth, had the means to shape the future of finance.

The importance of merchants and their role in the economy also helped give rise to a new middle class, distinct from the old feudal hierarchy of nobles and peasants. This middle class, composed of skilled artisans, tradespeople, and financiers, grew in both numbers and influence. They became the bedrock of the new urban economies, often forming guilds and associations that promoted their interests and ensured their economic survival.

In addition to the rise of the merchant class, the Black Death and its aftermath also created opportunities for more individuals to acquire land and wealth. The disruption of feudal labor systems meant that many peasants, who had previously been bound to the land as serfs, were able to negotiate better terms for their labor or even purchase land of their own. This shift from an agrarian-based economy to one dominated by urban centers and commerce laid the foundation for the modern economic world.

CHAPTER 6

Decline Of Feudalism And The Rise Of Land Ownership

The Black Death's impact on medieval Europe was not limited to the catastrophic loss of life; it triggered a seismic shift in the deeply entrenched feudal system that had long defined European society. The death of millions left vast tracts of land vacant, with many estates unable to operate without the labor of their peasants and serfs. The resulting labor shortages led to a dramatic decline in the economic and political power of the nobility, as they were unable to maintain the same level of control over their lands and tenants. Survivors, who suddenly found themselves in greater demand, leveraged their newfound bargaining power to negotiate higher wages, better working conditions, and even their freedom from servitude. The old bonds of fealty and obligation that had once tied peasants to their lords began to unravel, weakening the feudal hierarchy and giving rise to a more flexible, wage-based economy. For many, this newfound autonomy translated into opportunities to acquire and cultivate land of their own, reshaping the economic landscape.

As land ownership became more accessible, a new class of landowners began to emerge, fundamentally altering the social structure of medieval Europe. This transformation forced the traditional aristocracy to adapt or risk losing influence entirely. Many nobles, struggling to maintain their holdings, leased or sold land to commoners, reducing their control over agricultural production and redistributing wealth and influence in ways previously unthinkable. This shift also marked the beginning of a broader decline in noble power, as economic and political authority became increasingly decentralized. With greater opportunities for landownership and economic advancement, the rise of a more independent and prosperous class of freeholders laid the foundation for a more dynamic and modern society.

The Feudal System Eroded: Power Shifts in Europe

The feudal system that dominated Europe before the Black Death was a rigid hierarchy in which land was the primary measure of wealth and power. Nobles held large estates, and peasants, often bound as serfs, worked the land in exchange for protection. This system, while deeply hierarchical, provided stability to medieval society for centuries. However, the Black Death delivered a fatal blow to the structure upon which feudalism was built.

The plague decimated the population, wiping out nearly half of Europe's people. This unprecedented death toll led to a massive labor shortage across the continent, fundamentally altering the relationship between landowners and laborers. Before the plague, land was plentiful, and labor was cheap due to the abundance of peasants. After the plague, the scarcity of labor made surviving workers highly valuable, empowering them to negotiate better wages and working conditions. Serfs who had previously been tied to the land found themselves with more bargaining power. In many cases, they demanded (and received) higher wages or the freedom to move to other manors where conditions were better.

The result was a weakening of the bonds that held the feudal system together. Lords, desperate to retain their labor force, were often forced to offer concessions to their peasants, reducing the rigid class distinctions that defined feudal society. Across Europe, laws designed to keep wages artificially low or to restrict the movement of laborers—such as the Statute of Labourers enacted in England in 1351—proved largely ineffective. The socioeconomic changes unleashed by the plague were simply too powerful to be contained by legislation.

Furthermore, with fewer people to work the land, many nobles found themselves unable to maintain their large estates. Some were forced to lease or sell portions of their holdings to generate income, leading to a redistribution of land. This marked the beginning of the decline of the great feudal estates and the rise of a more diverse system of land ownership.

The Land Grab: Redistribution and New Landowners

As the feudal system weakened and the old order collapsed, a dramatic redistribution of land took place. The mass deaths caused by the Black Death left vast swathes of farmland unclaimed and abandoned. Nobles, desperate to hold on to their dwindling estates, often leased or sold land to commoners or to enterprising peasants who had managed to accumulate savings. This shift marked a departure from centuries of aristocratic land monopoly and created opportunities for new classes of landowners.

The redistribution of land allowed enterprising peasants and members of the emerging middle class to become landowners. In regions like England, the rise of "yeoman" farmers—wealthier peasants who owned their land—was a direct result of these changes. Yeoman farmers often operated independently, employing their own labor or leasing land to tenant farmers, thereby creating a more dynamic rural economy that was no longer strictly dependent on the rigid feudal hierarchy. The rise of a class of independent landowners also weakened the economic power of traditional nobles, who had previously controlled virtually all arable land.

In some regions, monasteries and the Church—historically among the largest landowners—also saw their holdings change hands. The plague did not spare the clergy; entire monastic communities were decimated, leaving many religious properties abandoned. Secular authorities often seized these lands, further accelerating the redistribution process. This not only diminished the Church's influence over land but also introduced new actors into the rural economy, who were more focused on profits and productivity than on maintaining feudal obligations.

The land grab and redistribution that followed the Black Death also had profound implications for agricultural practices. Many of the newly established small landholders experimented with more efficient farming techniques, as they were now responsible for maximizing the output and profitability of their land.

Some diversified their crops or shifted to pasture-based agriculture, especially in England, where a growing demand for wool led to the expansion of sheep farming. This agricultural innovation, driven by the new class of landowners, helped to spur economic growth and further weaken the old feudal order, which had been built on subsistence farming and strict social hierarchies.

Noble Decline: The Changing Role of Aristocracy

The decline of feudalism and the rise of individual landownership heralded a dramatic shift in the fortunes of the aristocracy. Before the plague, nobles derived their wealth and power primarily from their landholdings and the labor provided by peasants bound to the land. With the erosion of the feudal system and the redistribution of land, many nobles found themselves facing financial ruin. Their traditional sources of income dried up, and many were forced to adapt to a rapidly changing economic landscape.

In some cases, the decline of noble power was gradual. Many nobles continued to wield influence and retain some of their landholdings, but they had to contend with the demands of a more assertive peasantry and the growing power of the emerging merchant class. The days of unquestioned aristocratic dominance were over; nobles were now one of many competing interests in a rapidly evolving social and economic order.

One of the key challenges facing the nobility was the erosion of their labor force. The shortage of peasants, combined with the newfound freedom of many laborers to move and seek better opportunities, forced nobles to compete for workers. In some cases, they offered higher wages or more favorable terms to attract laborers, which led to increased costs and reduced profits. Nobles who failed to adapt often fell into debt, losing their estates to creditors or selling off their land piecemeal.

For those nobles who managed to maintain their estates, life after the Black Death often involved a shift in focus from land-based wealth to other forms of economic activity. Some nobles turned to commerce, investing in trade, banking, or emerging industries. The integration of nobles into the commercial economy marked a significant departure from the purely agrarian focus of the feudal system and signaled the rise of a more flexible and diverse economic elite.

The weakening of noble power was further compounded by changes in military technology and tactics. The feudal system had been built on a model of localized military service, with lords providing armed retainers in exchange for land grants. However, the rise of professional armies, financed by taxation rather than feudal obligations, gradually rendered this model obsolete. Monarchs, who sought to consolidate their power and establish more centralized states, no longer relied solely on the military support of the nobility. This shift further diminished the political power of the aristocracy.

In regions where city-states emerged as powerful political entities, such as Italy, the role of the traditional nobility was even more drastically altered. Wealthy merchant families, who had risen to prominence through trade and banking, often surpassed the old nobility in terms of economic and political influence. In cities like Florence and Venice, the power of the merchant elite eclipsed that of the traditional aristocracy, creating new forms of government and governance that were more responsive to the needs of commerce and industry.

The decline of noble power also had significant cultural and social implications. The old feudal ideals of chivalry and aristocratic privilege gave way to new values that emphasized individual achievement, merit, and economic success. This shift in values was reflected in the art, literature, and philosophy of the Renaissance, which celebrated human potential and the accomplishments of individuals rather than the rigid hierarchies of the medieval past.

At the same time, the decline of noble power was not uniform across Europe. In some regions, particularly in Eastern Europe, feudalism persisted for centuries after the Black Death, albeit in a modified form. The resilience of feudal structures in these regions was due in part to differences in population density, economic conditions, and political structures. However, even in these areas, the seeds of change sown by the Black Death would eventually bear fruit, leading to gradual shifts in social and economic relations.

CHAPTER 7

Seeds Of Nationalism Amidst Crisis

The Black Death's devastation of 14th-century Europe set off a chain reaction of social, economic, and political changes that would ultimately give rise to early forms of nationalism and the emergence of modern nation-states. The plague's staggering mortality rates weakened the traditional feudal bonds that had long governed daily life, while also undermining the universal authority of the Church, which had struggled to protect the populace or provide meaningful explanations for the suffering. In the face of such chaos, communities sought new sources of stability and cohesion. As the power of local lords waned, rulers and monarchs began to consolidate power, strengthening central governance, fostering local loyalty, and forging more cohesive national identities. The emergence of stronger central authority became a unifying force that gave rise to symbols, traditions, and languages that would ultimately evolve into a sense of shared national identity.

This burgeoning sense of nationalism was further fueled by shifts in military and civic obligations, as people became more willing to rally behind a unified state rather than decentralized feudal allegiances. Armies composed of loyal citizens began to replace the feudal levies once controlled by nobility, strengthening the centralized power of emerging nation-states. Economic changes also played a role; the redistribution of wealth and the growth of new social classes, such as the burgeoning middle class, created a new economic order that often prioritized national interests. Over time, loyalty to secular authorities began to outweigh religious allegiances, especially as monarchs positioned themselves as protectors of their people's welfare. By examining these shifts, this chapter delves into how the Black Death not only weakened existing institutions but also laid the groundwork for the development of stronger, more cohesive nation-states that would shape the trajectory of European history for centuries to come.

Emerging National Pride and Identity

Before the Black Death, most people in Europe defined themselves by their local identities, family, religious affiliations, and loyalty to a feudal lord. However, the unprecedented scale of the plague and its ensuing chaos made people reconsider their allegiances and identities. The widespread death and destruction created shared experiences of loss, fear, and hope across different regions, leading to a gradual but significant shift in self-perception and collective identity.

In many regions, the decline of feudal structures weakened the bonds between local lords and their subjects. The Black Death left many estates in disarray, often with no clear successor to the title and power held by deceased nobility. This eroded the traditional feudal allegiances that tied peasants to their land and lords, and communities began to think of themselves as part of larger regional or cultural entities. This was a critical step in the development of a broader, more cohesive sense of national identity.

During and after the plague, monarchs and rulers recognized the need to unify and rally their subjects to maintain order and protect their territories. Many took advantage of this situation to consolidate their power and promote a sense of unity under their leadership. For example, in England, the monarchy sought to project itself as a unifying force for the kingdom, emphasizing symbols and narratives that would foster loyalty to the Crown and a shared English identity. The Hundred Years' War with France, which overlapped with the time of the Black Death, further bolstered English nationalism as people united against a common enemy.

In France, the devastation wrought by the plague led to similar sentiments. Despite internal divisions, regional leaders and monarchs pushed for a sense of French identity and unity in response to the external threat posed by the English. The trauma of the Black Death provided a catalyst for this process, as communities sought stability and protection amidst the chaos.

The Black Death also played a role in reshaping cultural identity. Artists, writers, and chroniclers of the time documented the experiences of their communities, often reflecting a newfound appreciation for collective survival and resilience. Literature and chronicles that celebrated local and regional heroes became popular, laying the groundwork for later expressions of nationalism.

From the Church to the State: New Loyalties

The widespread death and suffering caused by the Black Death shook people's faith in the Church. At a time when religious institutions were supposed to provide solace and answers, many clergy succumbed to the disease, leaving their congregations without spiritual guidance. Moreover, the Church's inability to prevent or cure the plague undermined its credibility and authority. Some clergy exploited the crisis for personal gain, further tarnishing the reputation of religious institutions. This widespread disillusionment led many to question the Church's power and seek new sources of stability and loyalty.

Secular rulers, sensing an opportunity, sought to fill this vacuum by offering leadership and protection to their people. Monarchs and local leaders began to assert their authority more forcefully, positioning themselves as the rightful protectors and representatives of their territories. This shift in loyalty from religious to secular authorities was crucial in the gradual development of early nation-states. The rise of centralized monarchies, which demanded allegiance from their subjects, laid the foundation for a new political order in which loyalty to the state and ruler took precedence over allegiance to the Church.

In England, King Edward III capitalized on this changing dynamic by emphasizing his role as a protector and unifier. He strengthened his control over regional lords and promoted English law and customs as symbols of national identity. Across the Channel, in France, King Charles V and his successors pursued a similar agenda, consolidating power and fostering a sense of unity that transcended local loyalties.

This transition from religious to secular loyalty was not without resistance. In many areas, religious movements emerged to challenge both the Church and secular authorities. Heretical groups, such as the Lollards in England and the Hussites in Bohemia, criticized the Church's corruption and demanded reforms. While these movements were often suppressed, they reflected the changing loyalties of the time and the waning influence of traditional religious authority.

As secular rulers asserted their authority, they also began to institutionalize their power through laws, taxation, and military service. This helped create a sense of belonging and loyalty to the state, rather than to individual lords or the Church. Over time, these developments laid the groundwork for the modern concept of the nation-state, in which people identified with a centralized government and a common national identity.

Nation-States Formed from Disarray

The upheaval caused by the Black Death provided a fertile ground for the emergence of nascent nation-states. As feudal bonds weakened and new loyalties emerged, rulers sought to consolidate their territories and establish centralized systems of governance. This process was not uniform across Europe, but in many regions, the seeds of modern nation-states were sown.

One of the key factors driving the formation of nation-states was the need for effective governance in the aftermath of the plague. With so many dead, including members of the nobility and clergy, rulers had to find new ways to maintain control over their lands. Centralized administrations, often staffed by educated bureaucrats and advisors, became increasingly important. These officials helped enforce laws, collect taxes, and administer justice, creating a more unified and cohesive state apparatus.

In some regions, the rise of professional armies further strengthened the power of centralized states. The decline of the feudal levy system, in which nobles provided soldiers for military campaigns, led to the development of standing armies loyal to the monarch. This shift allowed rulers to project their power more effectively and maintain control over their territories. It also fostered a sense of loyalty and identity tied to the state, as soldiers fought not for individual lords, but for the nation as a whole.

The Hundred Years' War between England and France is a prime example of how military conflict contributed to the emergence of nation-states. The war, which was fueled in part by territorial disputes and dynastic claims, became a rallying point for both English and French nationalism. In England, victories such as the Battle of Agincourt in 1415 were celebrated as national triumphs, while in France, figures like Joan of Arc became symbols of resistance and national unity. The war helped solidify national identities and fostered a sense of collective loyalty to the state.

The formation of nation-states was also influenced by economic changes brought about by the Black Death. The decline of feudalism and the rise of a market-based economy created new opportunities for trade and commerce. Merchants and artisans, who were often excluded from the feudal system, found themselves in a position to influence political and economic decisions. In many cases, they allied themselves with monarchs and centralized governments, supporting policies that promoted stability and economic growth.

In Italy, the rise of city-states such as Florence, Venice, and Milan demonstrated how economic power could translate into political influence. These city-states, which were governed by powerful merchant families, developed sophisticated systems of governance that emphasized civic pride, economic success, and political autonomy. While not nation-states in the modern sense, they represented a departure from the fragmented feudal order and foreshadowed the emergence of centralized states.

The process of nation-state formation was not without conflict. In many regions, local nobles resisted the centralization of power, leading to rebellions and power struggles. However, over time, the power of centralized authorities grew stronger, aided by the development of legal systems, taxation policies, and military structures that reinforced their control. The emergence of nation-states was a gradual and often contentious process, but it marked a significant step in the evolution of European society.

CHAPTER 8

A Church Under Siege

The Black Death exposed deep vulnerabilities within the medieval Church, shaking the foundations of religious authority that had long provided spiritual and social cohesion for Europe's population. When the plague arrived, it struck indiscriminately, killing clergy and laity alike and leaving many people desperate for answers and reassurance. Initially, the Church attempted to provide guidance through prayers, masses, and penitential processions, but as the death toll mounted and miraculous cures failed to appear, many lost faith in the Church's power and its ability to intercede on behalf of humanity. The widespread death of clergy left parishes abandoned or poorly served, further eroding confidence in an institution that had once seemed all-powerful. Survivors were often haunted by doubt, questioning why God would allow such devastation and why the Church, supposedly His representative on Earth, appeared powerless. This spiritual crisis gave rise to a range of new religious expressions, such as the flagellant movement, which sought divine forgiveness through extreme public penance.

Amid this turbulence, the seeds of anti-clericalism and dissent took root, driven by growing disillusionment with Church leadership's corruption, greed, and perceived failures. Reports of clergy charging exorbitant fees for last rites, abandoning their posts, or living in excess during a time of widespread suffering exacerbated resentment among the faithful. This discontent would persist beyond the plague years, fueling critiques of Church practices and fostering reform movements that sought to address its shortcomings. The rise of heretical groups and calls for greater piety and ecclesiastical reform signaled a shift in religious life that would ultimately contribute to larger upheavals, such as the Protestant Reformation in the 16th century. The Black Death thus reshaped not only the physical and social landscape of Europe but also deeply altered its spiritual contours, setting the stage for centuries of religious transformation and conflict.

Faith in Crisis: The Church's Struggles to Respond

For medieval Europeans, the Church was more than a religious institution—it was the cornerstone of daily life, spiritual guidance, and social stability. When the Black Death began its deadly march across Europe in 1347, people turned to the Church for explanations and solace.

However, the clergy found themselves just as vulnerable to the disease as the rest of society, and their initial responses reflected the limits of both medieval understanding and institutional capacity.

In many regions, the mortality rate among clergy was staggeringly high; priests, monks, and nuns perished in droves as they ministered to the sick and dying. The Church's spiritual leaders, who were expected to provide comfort and divine intervention, often succumbed themselves, leaving parishes without guidance. The sudden death of so many clergy created a severe shortage of experienced spiritual leaders. In some areas, desperate communities ordained hastily chosen or poorly trained replacements, leading to a drop in the overall quality of religious instruction and care.

The Church's inability to stop the plague or offer effective explanations weakened its hold on the populace. Many clergymen interpreted the Black Death as divine punishment for sin, urging mass repentance and acts of piety. Public processions, penitential rituals, and fervent prayer campaigns were organized, but as the plague raged on unabated, disillusionment grew. People began to question why their prayers went unanswered and why God allowed such suffering to persist. The perceived failure of the Church to provide protection or clear answers shook people's faith and undermined its spiritual authority.

The pandemic also exposed instances of corruption and self-interest within the Church. While many clergy showed immense bravery, tending to the sick at great personal risk, others abandoned their posts out of fear or focused on amassing wealth. Wealthy individuals donated lavish sums to monasteries and churches in hopes of securing divine favor, but some religious leaders exploited these gifts for personal gain. This behavior fueled public resentment and contributed to growing suspicions about the Church's moral integrity.

Transforming Faith: New Religious Beliefs and Practices

Amid the spiritual crisis brought on by the Black Death, new religious practices and beliefs began to take shape. The trauma of the pandemic led people to explore different forms of spirituality, seeking comfort and meaning outside traditional Church teachings. This period of transformation set the stage for significant shifts in religious life.

One prominent movement that arose during the Black Death was the Flagellant movement. Flagellants were groups of self-punishing penitents who traveled from town to town, publicly whipping themselves to atone for humanity's sins. They believed that their extreme acts of penance would appease God's wrath and halt the spread of the plague. While the movement initially gained widespread popularity, the Church soon condemned it as heretical, viewing the Flagellants' rejection of clerical authority as a threat. Nevertheless, the movement highlighted the desire for more personal and immediate forms of religious expression.

Mysticism also flourished during and after the Black Death. Individuals sought direct, personal experiences of the divine, bypassing established Church rituals. Mystics such as Meister Eckhart and later figures like Julian of Norwich offered spiritual insights rooted in personal visions and contemplative prayer. Their teachings emphasized a more intimate relationship with God, often challenging the hierarchical structure of the medieval Church.

In addition to mystical movements, lay religious practices grew in popularity. Devotional confraternities, groups of laypeople dedicated to charitable works and prayer, emerged in response to the suffering caused by the plague. These groups allowed ordinary people to take an active role in their spiritual lives, fostering a sense of community and purpose during difficult times. The proliferation of lay-driven religious activity reflected a desire for greater autonomy and connection in religious practice, further diminishing the Church's monopoly on spiritual life.

Another key aspect of religious transformation was a shift in artistic expression. Art and literature began to reflect themes of death, suffering, and the transience of life, often with a strong spiritual undertone. The "Danse Macabre," or "Dance of Death," depicted skeletons leading people of all social ranks to their graves, serving as a reminder of mortality and the fleeting nature of earthly power. Such works captured the anxiety and spiritual reckoning that defined the era, reminding people of their ultimate fate while urging them to consider the state of their souls.

Discontent and Dissent: The Roots of Anti-Clericalism

The Black Death did more than reveal cracks in the Church's authority; it also sowed the seeds of anti-clericalism that would eventually lead to widespread calls for reform. The perception that many clergymen had abandoned their posts, failed in their spiritual duties, or exploited the suffering of the population fueled anger and distrust. As communities struggled to rebuild in the aftermath of the plague, they began to challenge the Church's wealth, corruption, and moral integrity.

Anti-clerical sentiment found fertile ground in critiques of the Church's immense wealth. Many people resented the opulence of bishops and abbots, particularly in light of the suffering and poverty that plagued their communities. The Church's practice of selling indulgences—promises of reduced time in purgatory in exchange for money—became a focal point of outrage. The sense that spiritual benefits could be bought and sold struck many as a betrayal of true Christian values.

Criticism of clerical behavior also played a significant role in the growth of anti-clericalism. Tales of priests who abandoned their congregations, acted immorally, or prioritized their own wealth over their duties spread widely. The actions of corrupt clergy stood in stark contrast to the heroism of those who remained at their posts, tending to the sick at great personal risk. This disparity highlighted the failures within the Church's ranks and fueled calls for reform.

Prominent voices of dissent emerged during this period, seeking to address the Church's shortcomings. In England, John Wycliffe, a theologian and reformer, became a vocal critic of Church corruption and the power of the papacy. Wycliffe argued for a return to a simpler, more scripturally focused faith, and his followers, known as Lollards, advocated for reforms such as translating the Bible into vernacular languages so that laypeople could read it for themselves. Although Wycliffe's ideas were initially condemned by Church authorities, they would later inspire future reform movements, including the Protestant Reformation.

In Bohemia, a similar movement arose under the leadership of Jan Hus, who called for Church reform and denounced the excesses of the clergy. Hus's teachings gained a wide following, and he became a symbol of resistance against Church corruption. His execution in 1415 sparked a series of rebellions known as the Hussite Wars, demonstrating the deepening divide between reform-minded communities and the established Church.

These movements highlighted the growing rift between the Church and its disillusioned followers. As the medieval period drew to a close, the seeds of reform planted during the era of the Black Death would continue to grow, eventually culminating in the seismic changes of the Reformation.

CHAPTER 9

Medieval Medicine And Science In Crisis

The Black Death's onslaught exposed the limitations and fragility of medieval medical knowledge, placing physicians and scholars at the center of a desperate struggle for answers and solutions. At the time, medicine was rooted in ancient theories from Greek and Roman thinkers like Galen and Hippocrates, with a heavy reliance on humoral theory, which believed that an imbalance in bodily fluids caused disease. Consequently, treatments often included bloodletting, purging, and the application of herbal concoctions meant to restore balance. Physicians, lacking an understanding of infectious disease and its bacterial origins, attributed the plague to a range of causes, from astrological alignments and divine punishment to miasmas—foul air thought to carry disease. The rapid spread and high mortality of the plague overwhelmed medical practitioners, leaving many unable to keep up with the demand for care or offer effective remedies, resulting in frustration, fear, and distrust among the afflicted population.

Amid this crisis, the boundaries between science and superstition blurred as desperate communities turned to a variety of remedies, both logical and fantastical, in their search for hope and healing. While some individuals continued to rely on licensed physicians, many sought alternative healers, folk remedies, or religious interventions such as prayers, amulets, and flagellation. The sheer scale of suffering prompted a reevaluation of medical practices and sowed the seeds of future scientific inquiry, even if tangible progress was limited during the initial crisis. By exposing the inadequacy of traditional methods, the plague nudged society toward a more empirical approach to understanding disease. The beginnings of public health measures, such as quarantines and isolation of the sick, marked a slow but significant shift toward collective efforts to combat epidemics. This tension between entrenched beliefs and a nascent scientific spirit offers a compelling narrative of a world on the brink of transformation, driven by the desperate need to make sense of and survive an unprecedented catastrophe.

Understanding Disease: Medical Knowledge of the Time

Medieval medicine in the 14th century was rooted in classical theories inherited from ancient Greek and

Roman texts, particularly those of Hippocrates and Galen. Central to medical practice was the belief in the four humors—blood, phlegm, yellow bile, and black bile. Health was understood as a balance among these humors, and disease was thought to result from an imbalance. This framework, combined with the lack of empirical observation, meant that many medical theories relied heavily on speculation and tradition rather than experimentation and evidence.

The causes of disease were often attributed to miasma, or "bad air," believed to emanate from decaying matter, swamps, and other foul environments. This miasmatic theory led people to carry aromatic herbs, wear protective masks, and burn incense to ward off harmful vapors. Another widespread belief was that celestial phenomena—such as the alignment of planets or the appearance of comets—could influence disease outbreaks. Astrological charts were consulted by physicians to determine the causes and cures for illnesses.

Religion also played a central role in understanding disease. Many medieval people believed that the plague was a punishment sent by God for their sins, requiring spiritual remedies such as prayer, penance, and pilgrimages. Religious interpretations often shaped both personal and communal responses to illness. Flagellant movements, in which groups publicly whipped themselves to atone for humanity's sins, emerged as a manifestation of collective guilt and desperation.

Faced with the rapid spread of the Black Death, medical practitioners struggled to apply these traditional theories to a disease that defied all known categories. The plague's symptoms, including high fever, chills, vomiting, boils, and rapid death, often baffled even the most learned physicians. It soon became clear that existing theories and treatments were inadequate for addressing the crisis.

Breakthroughs and Missteps: Emerging Treatments

The medical response to the Black Death was a mix of innovation, desperation, and adherence to ancient traditions. Physicians and healers experimented with a variety of treatments, ranging from herbal remedies to complex rituals designed to balance the humors. While many approaches were ineffective or even harmful, the crisis spurred some advances in medical thinking that laid the groundwork for later developments.

Among the most common treatments for the plague were bloodletting and purging. Physicians believed that removing "excess" blood or expelling other bodily fluids could restore balance to the humors. Bloodletting was typically performed by making small incisions in the skin or using leeches to draw out blood. Unfortunately, this practice often weakened patients further, leaving them more vulnerable to infection. Purging, which involved inducing vomiting or diarrhea, was similarly based on the belief that disease could be expelled from the body. Both methods reflected the limitations of humoral theory in addressing infectious disease.

Herbal medicine was widely practiced, and some remedies offered temporary relief or comfort. Physicians recommended mixtures of garlic, vinegar, and other herbs believed to have protective or cleansing properties. Theriac, a compound originally developed as an antidote to poison in antiquity, became a popular treatment for the plague due to its reputation as a "universal cure." Despite its complexity—theriac often contained dozens of ingredients—there is little evidence to suggest it had any real efficacy against the Black Death.

In response to the plague's airborne nature, medieval people sought to purify the air around them. Aromatic herbs such as rosemary, thyme, and lavender were burned in homes and public spaces. Physicians carried "plague masks" stuffed with fragrant substances to filter the air they breathed while treating patients. These measures, although based on flawed theories of miasma, reflected a rudimentary understanding of disease transmission and would later influence the development of quarantine practices.

Quarantine measures, in fact, represent one of the more effective responses to the Black Death. In port cities such as Venice, officials imposed a 40-day isolation period (quaranta giorni, from which we derive the word "quarantine") on ships and travelers suspected of carrying the plague. Although the mechanisms of disease transmission were poorly understood, these early attempts to contain outbreaks demonstrated a growing recognition of the need for public health interventions.

Amid the chaos, some physicians began to question traditional medical theories and seek new explanations for the disease. Observations of plague victims and the rapid spread of the illness prompted a shift toward empirical investigation. While progress was slow and often met with resistance from entrenched authorities, the seeds of a more scientific approach to medicine were being sown.

Science vs. Superstition: The Quest to Understand the Plague

The struggle to understand and combat the Black Death highlighted the tension between scientific inquiry and superstition in medieval Europe. Faced with an unprecedented crisis, people sought explanations from every available source—religion, astrology, folklore, and emerging scientific theories. This convergence of beliefs created a complex and often contradictory landscape of responses.

Superstition played a significant role in how communities interpreted and reacted to the plague. Many believed that witches, Jews, or other marginalized groups were responsible for spreading the disease through magical or malevolent means. Pogroms and violence against Jewish communities erupted in several regions, fueled by fear and scapegoating. These tragic episodes underscore the extent to which irrational fears and prejudices were exacerbated by the pandemic.

Amulets, charms, and protective talismans became popular among those seeking to ward off the plague. People carried objects believed to possess magical properties, such as written prayers or symbols, in hopes of protecting themselves from harm. The reliance on such items reflected the deep sense of helplessness felt by many in the face of the pandemic.

At the same time, the crisis inspired some to pursue more systematic approaches to understanding disease. Scholars and physicians began to collect data on the spread of the plague, recording observations about symptoms, mortality rates, and patterns of transmission. While much of this work was limited by contemporary medical knowledge, it represented an early attempt to apply empirical methods to the study of infectious disease.

One of the key figures in this emerging scientific approach was Guy de Chauliac, a French surgeon who treated plague victims and documented his observations. Chauliac's writings reflect both the limitations and potential of medieval medicine; while he adhered to humoral theory, he also recognized the contagious nature of the disease and advocated for practical measures such as isolation of the sick. His work exemplifies the blend of tradition and innovation that characterized the medical response to the Black Death.

In the years following the plague, medical and scientific thinking continued to evolve. The experience of the pandemic underscored the need for better methods of disease prevention and treatment, leading to gradual shifts in medical education and practice. The foundations of modern epidemiology and public health were laid as physicians and scholars sought to understand the causes and transmission of disease more thoroughly.

The Black Death also had a profound impact on scientific inquiry beyond medicine. The devastation wrought by the plague prompted a broader reevaluation of natural philosophy, encouraging scholars to question established doctrines and seek new explanations for the natural world. This spirit of inquiry would eventually contribute to the intellectual transformations of the Renaissance and the Scientific Revolution.

CHAPTER 10

The Lasting Impact Of The Black Death

The Black Death's impact reached far beyond the death and chaos it inflicted, setting off ripples that would shape European history for generations. The mass mortality created severe labor shortages that upended feudal economies reliant on rigid hierarchies and serfdom. As survivors leveraged their newfound scarcity to demand better wages and conditions, traditional feudal bonds weakened, creating space for a burgeoning class of wage earners and new economic opportunities. The disruption of trade and commerce, once catastrophic, gradually stimulated innovative economic practices and laid the groundwork for a more diversified, market-driven society. With power dynamics shifting and established norms challenged, society adapted in response, laying the seeds for more equitable labor relationships and altering the distribution of wealth and resources in ways that would profoundly shape Europe's future trajectory.

Culturally and intellectually, the Black Death served as a stark reminder of human mortality, prompting deep reflection and catalyzing advancements in thought, art, and scientific exploration. In the wake of mass suffering, people began to question traditional institutions, particularly the Church, whose perceived inadequacies during the crisis led to growing dissatisfaction and a push for reform. Art and literature, too, evolved, capturing the fragility of life and the resilience of the human spirit, thus contributing to the flourishing of the Renaissance. The Black Death demonstrated the necessity of adaptive responses to crisis, offering lessons that resonate today in the face of modern pandemics: from the importance of resilient social systems to proactive health measures and global cooperation. The plague's legacy thus endures as both a cautionary tale of human vulnerability and a testament to the resilience and transformative power inherent in times of great adversity.

From Plague to Progress: Social and Economic Legacies

The death toll of the Black Death was staggering, with estimates placing the mortality rate at anywhere from 30% to 60% of Europe's population. Entire villages were wiped out, cities were left with decimated populations, and social structures were thrown into chaos. Yet, out of this tragedy emerged profound social and economic changes that reshaped the trajectory of European history.

- **Economic Shifts and the End of Feudalism**

One of the most significant long-term impacts of the Black Death was the erosion of the feudal system. Before the plague, most of Europe operated under a rigid feudal hierarchy in which peasants, or serfs, were bound to the land and owed allegiance to local lords. The sudden and massive loss of life upended this system. With so many laborers dead, surviving peasants found themselves in a position to demand better wages, improved working conditions, and even personal freedom. Many serfs fled their manorial lands to seek work elsewhere, further destabilizing the feudal order.

The labor shortage led to rising wages for workers and a shift in economic power away from the nobility and toward the emerging class of free laborers and skilled artisans. This period of economic upheaval paved the way for the growth of a wage-based economy and contributed to the decline of serfdom across much of Europe. In many regions, landlords attempted to resist these changes by enforcing harsh labor laws and fixing wages, but such efforts often sparked peasant revolts, underscoring the deep social tensions unleashed by the plague.

The redistribution of wealth and changes in labor dynamics also fostered a climate of innovation. As workers became scarcer and more valuable, there was greater incentive to adopt labor-saving technologies and improve agricultural and manufacturing processes. These developments laid the groundwork for economic growth in the centuries that followed.

- **Changes in Land Ownership and Rural Society**

The plague's impact on land ownership was another critical factor in reshaping medieval society. With so many landowners dead, vast tracts of land were left vacant or fell into the hands of new owners. In some cases, wealthy merchants or newly freed peasants were able to acquire land, breaking the traditional monopoly of the aristocracy. This redistribution of land ownership marked a significant shift in rural society, allowing for greater social mobility and the rise of a more diverse landholding class.

These changes contributed to the gradual emergence of a more market-oriented economy, as landowners sought to maximize profits by shifting from subsistence farming to cash crops and engaging in commercial agriculture. The development of new agricultural techniques, including crop rotation and improved plowing methods, also helped increase productivity. The economic landscape of

Europe was becoming more diverse and dynamic, setting the stage for future growth.

Fueling the Renaissance: The Cultural Impact of Tragedy

The social and economic shifts triggered by the Black Death had profound cultural repercussions that reverberated through the Renaissance, a period of renewed interest in art, science, literature, and humanism. In many ways, the Black Death served as a catalyst for this cultural awakening by challenging traditional norms and inspiring new ways of thinking.

- **A New Outlook on Life and Death**

The experience of mass death and widespread suffering profoundly shaped the psyche of medieval Europeans. The fragility of life became a central theme in art, literature, and philosophy, as people grappled with the suddenness and indiscriminate nature of the plague. This preoccupation with mortality is evident in the art of the period, with motifs such as the "Danse Macabre" (Dance of Death) illustrating the universality of death and the fleeting nature of earthly life. While grim, this focus on mortality also sparked a desire to celebrate life, leading to a cultural shift toward individualism and self-expression.

The Church, which had long been the dominant authority in spiritual and intellectual matters, faced significant challenges to its power and influence during and after the plague. The inability of religious leaders to provide effective answers or relief during the crisis led to widespread disillusionment with traditional religious practices and institutions. This crisis of faith created space for new religious movements, philosophical inquiry, and secular thinking, all of which contributed to the intellectual ferment of the Renaissance.

- **Artistic and Intellectual Flourishing**

The Black Death also had a direct impact on the patronage of the arts. Wealthy survivors of the plague, including members of the burgeoning merchant class, often sought to commemorate their experiences and express their piety through artistic commissions. This increase in patronage fueled the creation of masterpieces by artists such as Giotto, who depicted human emotion and suffering with unprecedented realism. The emphasis on human experience and emotion in art reflected broader changes in society's understanding of the human condition.

In addition to the visual arts, the spread of humanism—a Renaissance movement focused on the study of classical texts and the value of individual human achievement—was shaped by the aftermath of the plague. Humanist scholars sought to reconcile traditional beliefs with new ways of thinking, laying the groundwork for advances in science, literature, and philosophy. Figures such as Petrarch, who lived through the plague, captured the tension between medieval and modern worldviews in their writings.

Lessons for Today: Insights for Modern Pandemic Response

The legacy of the Black Death offers valuable lessons for contemporary society, particularly in the context of modern pandemics and public health crises. The experience of the 14th-century pandemic underscores the importance of effective communication, public health measures, and social resilience in the face of disease outbreaks. While the world has changed dramatically since the days of the Black Death, certain fundamental challenges remain relevant.

- **Public Health and Quarantine Measures**

One of the most effective responses to the Black Death was the use of quarantine to contain the spread of the disease. Port cities such as Venice pioneered quarantine measures, isolating ships and travelers for 40 days to prevent the introduction of plague into the population. This early form of public health intervention highlights the value of containment and isolation in controlling infectious diseases—principles that continue to guide modern responses to pandemics.

The importance of timely and transparent communication during a health crisis cannot be overstated. During the Black Death, the spread of misinformation, fear, and superstition often exacerbated the crisis, leading to scapegoating and violence. Modern society faces similar challenges in combating misinformation and building public trust in health authorities. Effective communication, based on scientific evidence and delivered with empathy, remains a cornerstone of successful pandemic response.

- **Social and Economic Resilience**

The Black Death revealed both the fragility and resilience of medieval society. While the initial impact of the plague was devastating, communities found ways to adapt, rebuild, and even thrive in the aftermath. The economic transformations that followed the plague were driven by the need to adapt to new realities, including labor shortages and changing social norms. This spirit of adaptation and resilience is equally important in modern contexts, as societies grapple with the long-term effects of pandemics on economies, health systems, and social structures.

The unequal distribution of the plague's impact also highlights the importance of addressing social and economic disparities in pandemic response. Vulnerable populations, including the poor and marginalized, often bear the brunt of public health crises. Efforts to mitigate these disparities and ensure equitable access to resources, healthcare, and support systems are essential for building resilient and inclusive societies.

- **Science, Innovation, and Collaboration**

The Black Death spurred advances in medical knowledge, public health practices, and scientific inquiry, despite the limitations of medieval understanding. Today, the rapid development of vaccines, treatments, and public health strategies in response to pandemics such as COVID-19 demonstrates the power of scientific collaboration and innovation. The lessons of the past remind us that progress often arises from crisis and that the pursuit of knowledge and collaboration across borders is critical to overcoming global challenges.

CHAPTER 11

Regional Responses – A Closer Look

The Black Death's impact across Europe was far from uniform; local responses were deeply influenced by each region's unique social, political, and economic conditions, illustrating the plague's wide-ranging influence on medieval society. In England, the massive population loss led to a significant decline in available labor, severely undermining the feudal system. Serfs and peasants, newly empowered by their scarcity, demanded higher wages and better working conditions, leading to widespread social unrest, exemplified by the Peasants' Revolt of 1381. The English nobility, weakened by the crisis, faced a redistribution of power as landholdings changed hands and new wealth dynamics emerged. This shift permanently altered the relationship between landowners and laborers, signaling the gradual decline of serfdom and giving rise to a more mobile and economically empowered peasant class.

In Italy, where dense urban populations facilitated the rapid spread of the plague, responses varied among city-states but often resulted in profound political and cultural changes. The sudden collapse of families and the loss of skilled workers disrupted commerce, forcing cities like Florence and Venice to adapt rapidly. The crisis led to new public health measures, including the establishment of quarantine zones, which marked the early development of modern public health practices. Economically, the merchant class—integral to the prosperity of these city-states—faced challenges but ultimately adapted, fueling economic innovation and recovery. France, meanwhile, contended with the simultaneous pressures of the plague and the ongoing Hundred Years' War, which exacerbated its social and economic strain. The monarchy's response focused on centralizing authority, which, coupled with the weakening grip of the nobility, paved the way for the gradual emergence of a more unified nation-state. By exploring these regional differences, we uncover the diverse ways in which the Black Death reshaped European society, highlighting both the resilience and adaptability of its people and the unique paths of recovery that would influence their trajectories for centuries to come.

England: Noble Shifts and Peasant Revolts

In England, the Black Death accelerated the erosion of the feudal system, which had already been under strain before the pandemic. The massive loss of life led to severe labor shortages, giving surviving peasants and serfs newfound leverage in their relationships with landowners. With a significant portion of the workforce gone, landowners had to compete for laborers, often offering higher wages and better conditions to attract workers. Many peasants used this opportunity to demand their freedom from traditional feudal obligations, such as labor service and high rents.

The English government, under the influence of the nobility, attempted to counter these changes by enacting harsh labor laws designed to maintain the status quo. The Ordinance of Labourers in 1349 and the Statute of Labourers in 1351 sought to freeze wages at pre-plague levels and prevent laborers from moving in search of better pay. These efforts, however, were met with resistance and ultimately failed to stop the tide of social change sweeping the countryside.

- **The Peasants' Revolt of 1381**

The strain between landowners and laborers boiled over into open conflict in 1381 with the Peasants' Revolt, one of the most significant uprisings in medieval English history. While the revolt had multiple causes—including heavy taxation and political grievances—the economic discontent stemming from the Black Death was a critical driver. Led by figures such as Wat Tyler and John Ball, the rebels marched on London, demanding an end to serfdom, lower taxes, and greater social and economic freedoms.

Although the revolt was ultimately crushed by King Richard II's forces, it marked a turning point in English society. The government realized that maintaining the rigid pre-plague order was impossible. Over time, many of the peasants' demands were met through gradual reforms and negotiations, leading to a decline in serfdom and the rise of a more mobile and empowered peasantry.

- **Noble Power and Land Redistribution**

The Black Death also affected England's nobility, as many aristocratic families were decimated by the plague. With fewer heirs to inherit estates, significant landholdings changed hands, sometimes passing to new families or consolidating under fewer owners. This shift in land ownership altered the balance of power within the nobility and contributed to the ongoing transformation of England's social and political landscape.

Italy: City-States and the Rise of Commerce

Italy's geography and economic structure made it particularly vulnerable to the Black Death. As a region dominated by wealthy and densely populated city-states, including Florence, Venice, and Genoa, Italy's urban centers became hotspots for the plague's rapid spread. Trade routes linking Italy to the rest of Europe and beyond facilitated the movement of goods and people— and with them, disease. When the Black Death struck, these cities faced immense challenges in containing the outbreak and managing its devastating effects.

- **Economic Adaptation and Commercial Innovation**

Despite the initial shock, many Italian city-states proved remarkably resilient in their responses to the Black Death. The economic structure of these cities, based on commerce, banking, and skilled craftsmanship, allowed for a quicker recovery compared to more rural regions. Merchants and entrepreneurs adapted to the new economic reality by diversifying their investments, expanding trade networks, and adopting new business practices.

One notable response was the growth of banking and financial services, as merchants sought to rebuild their fortunes and finance new ventures. Prominent families, such as the Medici in Florence, capitalized on these opportunities, eventually becoming influential patrons of art and culture during the Renaissance. The wealth generated by commercial activity also allowed city-states to invest in public infrastructure, including hospitals, orphanages, and public health initiatives designed to prevent future outbreaks.

- **Art and Cultural Flourishing**

The Black Death had a profound impact on Italian art and culture, contributing to the emergence of the Renaissance. Artists and writers grappled with themes of mortality, suffering, and human resilience, producing works that reflected both the horrors of the plague and the renewed sense of human potential that followed. The patronage of wealthy survivors fueled artistic and architectural endeavors, transforming Italy's cityscapes and laying the cultural foundations for a period of unprecedented creativity and intellectual exploration.

- **Civic Governance and Public Health**

Italy's city-states were also notable for their early public health responses to the Black Death. Cities like Venice pioneered quarantine measures, establishing isolated hospitals known as "lazzaretti" for plague victims. These measures, though imperfect, represented some of the earliest efforts to manage infectious disease through organized public health initiatives. The emphasis on civic governance and the collective good became a hallmark of Italian responses to the plague and reflected the resilience and adaptability of the region's urban populations.

France: Monarchical Power and Religious Authority

In France, the Black Death struck at a time of political instability and ongoing conflict, including the Hundred Years' War with England. The sudden loss of life weakened both the peasantry and the nobility, creating opportunities for the French monarchy to consolidate power. King Charles VI and subsequent rulers sought to strengthen royal authority, using the chaos of the plague to undermine feudal lords and centralize control over the realm.

The monarchy's efforts to exert greater control often led to tension with local lords and other power brokers. In some regions, attempts to impose new taxes or assert royal authority sparked resistance and unrest. The complex interplay between monarchs, nobles, and commoners during and after the plague shaped the evolution of French governance and laid the groundwork for future conflicts over the balance of power.

- **Religious Responses and the Church's Role**

The Catholic Church played a central role in France's response to the Black Death, offering spiritual guidance, organizing charitable efforts, and providing care for the sick. However, the Church's inability to halt the spread of the plague or offer meaningful solutions to the suffering led to widespread disillusionment. Many people questioned the Church's spiritual authority and sought alternative forms of religious expression.

Mystical and apocalyptic movements gained popularity, as did local saints' cults and lay religious associations that emphasized direct engagement with faith. While the Church retained significant influence, its moral and spiritual authority was increasingly challenged, contributing to the broader trend of anti-clericalism that would become more pronounced in the centuries to come.

- **Economic Challenges and Recovery Efforts**

France's economy was deeply affected by the Black Death, as agricultural production declined, trade routes were disrupted, and local markets faltered. The loss of laborers led to increased wages for surviving workers, but it also created tension between peasants and landowners. Many lords attempted to reinstate traditional labor obligations or impose higher rents, leading to peasant revolts and uprisings, such as the Jacquerie in 1358.

Over time, France's economy began to recover through a combination of labor reforms, market adaptation, and new agricultural practices. The Black Death's impact on land distribution and labor dynamics mirrored broader European trends, with long-term consequences for social and economic structures.

CONCLUSION

Reflections On A Shattered World

The Black Death left a scar on the face of medieval Europe unlike any other event in recorded history. It wiped out approximately one-third of the continent's population in the span of a few short years, plunging society into unimaginable turmoil. But this tragedy also acted as a powerful force of transformation, forever altering the social, economic, and cultural landscape of Europe. As we reflect on this shattered world, it becomes clear that the Black Death's impact extended far beyond the immediate suffering and devastation; it profoundly reshaped how societies functioned, redefined relationships between individuals and institutions, and ultimately laid the foundation for a modernizing Europe.

In the wake of the pandemic, survivors faced a world that was almost unrecognizable. Entire villages disappeared, towns were depopulated, and fields once brimming with laborers stood abandoned. The feudal system, with its rigid social hierarchies and economic structures, crumbled under the weight of widespread mortality and labor scarcity. Peasants, who were traditionally tied to the land and subjected to lords, found newfound leverage. In this radically altered world, labor became a precious commodity, and those who survived could demand better wages and conditions. The decline of serfdom, which had endured for centuries, was hastened by these changes, leading to the erosion of a system that had defined much of medieval Europe's economy.

As Europe began to recover, new economic models emerged from the ashes of the old. The shock of the Black Death accelerated the transition from a predominantly agrarian economy to one increasingly defined by commerce, trade, and urban growth. Merchants and craftsmen who survived the plague found themselves in a position of economic power, and many city-states flourished as centers of trade and innovation. This economic revitalization, however, was not without its challenges; inflation, deflation, and other forms of economic instability were common in the aftermath of the pandemic. Despite this, the seeds of a more diversified and resilient economy were sown, with long-term implications for Europe's development.

The social impact of the Black Death was equally profound. It upended traditional hierarchies and paved the way for increased social mobility. The rigid divisions between nobility, clergy, and commoners began to blur as new opportunities for wealth and influence emerged.

As survivors rebuilt their lives, they questioned the institutions that had once dominated medieval life, including the Church. The Church, whose authority was deeply intertwined with every aspect of life, was weakened by the plague. Its inability to protect the faithful from the ravages of the disease and its often self-serving behavior during the crisis led to widespread disillusionment and dissent. This weakening of ecclesiastical power laid the groundwork for reform movements that would reshape religious and political life for centuries to come.

In the midst of tragedy, the intellectual and cultural response to the Black Death was marked by both despair and resilience. Art and literature reflected the fear, sorrow, and hope that defined this era, capturing the fragility of human existence. Yet, this cultural reflection also spurred innovation and curiosity. As medieval medicine and science struggled to respond to the plague, a newfound spirit of inquiry emerged. This spirit, while still constrained by superstition and religious orthodoxy, planted the seeds of critical thought that would later blossom during the Renaissance. The Black Death thus served as both a brutal reminder of human vulnerability and a catalyst for intellectual growth.

As we look back on the Black Death from a modern perspective, it is impossible to ignore the echoes of this historical tragedy in our own time. Pandemics continue to test societies, revealing weaknesses in public health systems, economic disparities, and the resilience of social bonds. The Black Death reminds us of the importance of preparedness, cooperation, and compassion in the face of crisis. It also highlights humanity's remarkable ability to adapt and rebuild in the wake of unimaginable adversity. By learning from history, we gain valuable insight into the challenges and opportunities that arise during times of great upheaval.

The legacy of the Black Death is both a cautionary tale and a testament to human resilience. It reminds us that from great loss can come renewal and transformation. European society emerged from the ashes of this pandemic forever changed, with a greater sense of agency, new economic and social systems, and an emboldened spirit of inquiry. The people who survived the Black Death endured immense suffering but also laid the groundwork for a more modern Europe. Their struggles, resilience, and achievements offer us not only a window into a harrowing past but also lessons for navigating our own uncertain future.

The story of the Black Death is a story of survival against all odds. It is a story of despair, hope, loss, and renewal. As we reflect on this shattered world, we are reminded that history's greatest tragedies often carry within them the seeds of transformation. From the collapse of old orders came the possibility of new beginnings, and from immense suffering arose a more dynamic, adaptable society. In this way, the Black Death stands as a powerful symbol of both the fragility and the resilience of the human spirit, offering lessons that remain as relevant today as they were in the darkest days of the 14th century.

Reflecting on the aftermath of this devastating pandemic, we can appreciate the strength and adaptability of human communities in times of crisis. The Black Death reshaped the trajectory of European history, altering institutions, economies, and lives in ways that continue to resonate. It is a reminder that even in the face of overwhelming challenges, humanity has the capacity to rebuild, transform, and chart a new course for the future. This legacy, rooted in both tragedy and resilience, is what makes the history of the Black Death a timeless story of human perseverance and adaptation.

APPENDICES

Detailed Timeline of the Black Death

This timeline traces the journey of the Black Death, emphasizing its origins, spread, and major milestones across Europe. It provides a chronological overview that contextualizes the pandemic's far-reaching impact.

- **1338-1339**: Evidence suggests a plague outbreak in the Lake Issyk-Kul region in Central Asia. Burials in the area show high death rates from a disease resembling the bubonic plague.
- **1346:** The Black Death begins to move westward from Central Asia, spreading along trade routes. The outbreak reaches the Black Sea port of Kaffa (modern-day Feodosia in Crimea), a critical trade hub.

- **1347:** Genoese ships carrying infected passengers and rats arrive in Sicily, bringing the plague to Europe. The disease quickly spreads across Italian ports.

- **1348**: January The plague reaches Marseille in France.

- **Spring**: The outbreak spreads to Spain, Portugal, and Northern Italy.

- **Summer**: The plague crosses the English Channel and enters England through the port of Melcombe in Dorset. It spreads rapidly throughout the country.

- **Late 1348:** Paris, Bordeaux, Lyon, and London are severely affected.

- **1349**: The Black Death continues its devastating march through Europe: Scandinavia is struck, including Norway, Sweden, and Denmark.

- Rising anti-Semitic violence and pogroms against Jewish communities occur, as they are scapegoated for the plague.

- The pandemic intensifies its grip on Central Europe, including Germany and Austria.

- **1350:** The plague reaches Russia, entering from the western regions. Despite some areas being less affected, most major regions experience population loss and social disruption.

- **1351:** The plague subsides in many areas but remains present in some localized outbreaks. The cumulative death toll is estimated at 25 to 50 million people across Europe.

- **1353:** The initial wave of the Black Death is considered to have ended, though the disease would reappear in periodic outbreaks over subsequent centuries.

This timeline highlights key moments that illustrate how the Black Death reshaped the social and economic landscape of Europe, leaving scars that would endure for generations.

Glossary of Medieval Terms and Concepts

1. **Bubonic Plague**: A form of plague caused by the bacterium Yersinia pestis, characterized by swollen and painful lymph nodes (buboes), fever, chills, and other symptoms. It was the most common form of the disease during the Black Death.

2. **Clergy**: Members of the Church, including priests, monks, nuns, and other religious figures. The Church wielded immense power and influence in medieval society.

3. **Flagellant Movement**: Groups of religious zealots who believed the plague was God's punishment. They sought atonement through public displays of penance, such as whipping themselves.

4. **Feudal System:** The dominant social and economic structure in medieval Europe. It was based on a hierarchy of lords, vassals, and serfs, with obligations of land ownership, service, and protection.

5. **Guilds**: Associations of artisans and merchants who controlled the practice of their craft in a particular area. Guilds played a significant role in regulating commerce and maintaining trade standards.

6. **Miasma Theory**: The belief that diseases were spread by "bad air" or noxious fumes. This was a common explanation for the spread of the plague during the medieval period.

7. **Pogroms**: Organized attacks against Jewish communities, often fueled by prejudice, scapegoating, and economic tensions. Many Jewish people were falsely accused of causing the plague by poisoning wells.

8. **Serfdom**: The status of peasants under the feudal system. Serfs were tied to the land and obligated to provide labor or produce in exchange for protection and the right to work their lord's land.

9. **Quarantine**: A public health measure used to isolate individuals or ships suspected of carrying the plague. The practice originated during the Black Death, with ships in Venice required to remain in isolation for 40 days (from the Italian quaranta giorni).

10. **Sumptuary Laws**: Regulations intended to control consumption and display of wealth, particularly through clothing and luxury items. They were used to reinforce social hierarchies during and after the plague's upheaval.

Manufactured by Amazon.ca
Acheson, AB